The Illustrated
Acts of the Apostles

Jean-François Kieffer
Christine Ponsard

Translated by Janet Chevrier

The Illustrated
Acts of the Apostles

for Children

Ignatius

MAGNIFICAT®

"… She who was so good and did such good works …"
(see Acts 9:36)

To Agnès, Cécile, and Jean

After his resurrection, Jesus ascended to heaven next to his Father. Soon afterward, on the day of Pentecost, the apostles received from the Holy Spirit great power to proclaim the Gospel and to witness to the love of God for man. This is how the life of the first Christians—and the life of the Church—began.

Since that time, thousands, millions of men and women have continued to make Jesus known throughout the world. It is thanks to them that you can read this book today. It is also thanks to them, moreover, that you can live as a child of God, pray to Jesus, and love those around you.

Following Saint Peter, Saint Paul, and all the holy apostles, you can take your turn as a witness to the Gospel. May the breath of the Holy Spirit give you strength and courage!

TABLE OF CONTENTS

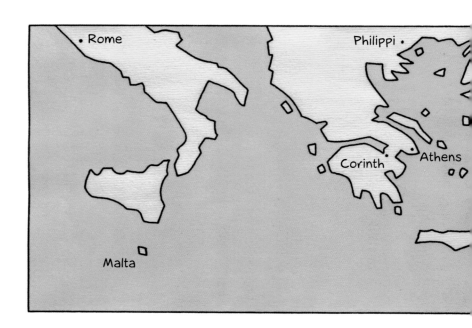

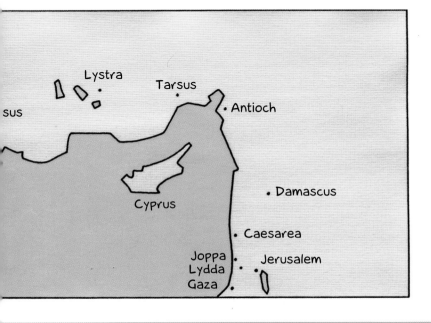

ASCENSION AND PENTECOST

Luke 24:49–53 and Acts 2:1–37

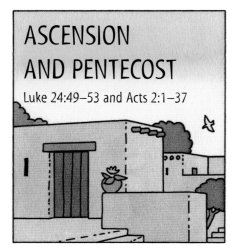

The risen Jesus announces to his disciples the coming of the Holy Spirit.

I will send upon you what my Father promised. Stay in Jerusalem until this power comes from on high . . .

Then he leads them near Bethany.

He raises his hands in blessing.

As he blesses them, he leaves them and is taken up to heaven.

The disciples retur to Jerusalem full of joy.

ll gather each
ay to pray with
ary and the other
iends of Jesus.

On the day of Pentecost, they suddenly hear a sound like a great gust of wind. They see what looks like tongues of fire settling on each of them.

They are filled with the Holy Spirit!

Alleluia!

Jesus is risen!

eter speaks to
e crowd:

et all the people
of Israel know:
this Jesus whom
ou crucified, God
made him Lord
and Christ!

All are moved at these words.

Brothers, what are we to do?

Change your hearts, be baptized in the name of Jesus Christ, and you will receive the Holy Spirit.

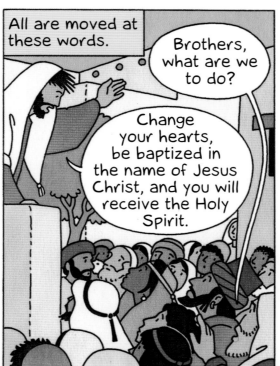

God promised it for you! For your children and for all those far off, for all whom God will call!

That day, three thousand people are baptized.

LIVING AS BROTHERS

Acts 2:42–47

After Pentecost, more and more people come to believe. They listen faithfully to the teachings of the apostles.

The Lord said, "Love your enemies" . . .

They live as brothers.

Justus has sold his field; the money will be shared among those in need!

THE BEGGAR AT THE GATE

Acts 3:1–16

Peter and John go up to the Temple for evening prayer. A man crippled from birth is sitting begging at the Beautiful Gate.

Alms, please!

Peter and John turn their gaze on him.

Look at us . . .

I have no money, but what I do have I give to you: in the name of Jesus Christ, rise and walk!

Peter takes him by the hand. In one leap, he stands up and walks!

THE APOSTLES BEFORE THE GREAT COUNCIL

Acts 5:27–42

Since the apostles never stop talking to the crowds about Jesus, the Temple guards arrest them and bring them before the great council . . .

Hearing these words, the chief priests become very angry.

But a Pharisee stands up:

Men of Israel, thi
carefully about wh
you are going to c
to these people . .

what they do comes from man, it will not last; but if it comes from God, you won't be able to stop it . . .

Don't run the risk of going to war against God himself!

You're right, Gamaliel . . .

Have them whipped, and then release them.

And don't speak about that man anymore!

But they leave full of joy that they have suffered for Jesus. And every day, in the Temple and in their homes, they spread the good news: Jesus is the Messiah!

SEVEN MEN TO SERVE

Acts 4:32–35 and 6:1–7

The believers share everything in common, distributing to each one according to his need. But soon . . .

Some are complaining they receive less than others . . .

Let's call a meeting of the disciples . . .

We, the Twelve,* shouldn't neglect preaching the Word of God in order to take care of the food . . .

Instead, choose from among you seven reputable men, filled with the Holy Spirit and wisdom. We will appoint them to this task.

Then we can devote our time to prayer and preaching the Gospel.

*Judas has been replaced by Matthias

16

The whole gathering is happy with the apostles' plan. They choose:

Stephen,

Philip,

Prochorus,

Nicanor,

Timon,

Parmenas,

Nicolaus

They are presented to the apostles. After praying, they lay hands on them.

THE MARTYRDOM OF STEPHEN

Acts 6:8—7:60

Stephen, who is full of the grace of God, works wonders.

I'm cured!

It's a miracle!

Glory to God!

But some become jealous of him . . .

Let's find false witnesses to accuse him!

This man is always speaking against God!

Is this true?

So Stephen reminds them of the story of the covenant between God and his people, from Abraham up to Jesus.

God made a covenant with you. But you are hardheaded! Your ears and your hearts don't want to listen to the Holy Spirit!

THE BAPTISM OF THE ETHIOPIAN

Acts 8:26–39

On the road from Jerusalem to Gaza, the Spirit of the Lord speaks to Philip.

Catch up with that chariot . . .

Returning from a trip to Jerusalem to worship God, an Ethiopian sits in the chariot reading the Book of Isaiah:

"Like a sheep he was led to the slaughter, like a silent lamb, he opened not his mouth . . ."

Do you understand what you're reading?

How can I, unless someone explains it to me?

Of whom is Isaiah speaking? Himself, or someone else?

So, starting from this text of the Bible, Philip proclaims to him the good news of Jesus.

Here is some water; what's to stop me from being baptized?

I baptize you in the name of the Father, and of the Son, and of the Holy Spirit.

When they come out of the water, Philip disappears from sight, and the Ethiopian goes on his way rejoicing.

♫ Jesus, you are my Savior. ♫

PAUL'S CONVERSION

Acts 9:1–30

Damascus, [P]aul goes without [fo]od and water.

After three days, a man comes to see him. It is Ananias, a disciple of the Lord.

Paul, my brother, it is the Lord Jesus who appeared to you on the road . . .

He sent me so that you might regain your sight and be filled with the Holy Spirit!

[W]ith that:

I . . . I can see!

Paul soon receives baptism.

He spends a few days with the disciples in Damascus and, without further delay, goes into the synagogues to proclaim that Jesus is the Son of God.

All who hear Paul are very surprised . . .

Jesus is the Son of God!

Isn't he the one who persecuted Jesus' disciples in Jerusalem?

And he came to Damascus to arrest them!

This traitor must die!

Don't let Paul leave Damascus!

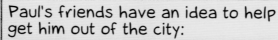

Paul's friends have an idea to help get him out of the city:

Climb into this basket.

May God keep you!

Paul returns to Jerusalem.

here he tries to join the group of disciples; but they are afraid of him.

Brothers . . .

It's Paul!

Run!

Then Barnabas introduces him to the apostles:

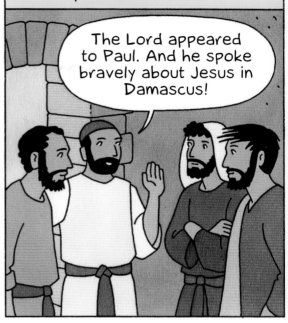

The Lord appeared to Paul. And he spoke bravely about Jesus in Damascus!

You are our brother.

Welcome among us.

Paul accompanies the disciples in the streets of Jerusalem and speaks powerfully to the Greek-speaking Jews.

Jesus, the Christ, is risen!

But some still seek to kill him, and he is forced to flee again. The brothers send him off to Tarsus, the city of his birth.

THE RAISING OF TABITHA

Acts 9:31–42

Through all Judea, Galilee, and Samaria, the Church lives in peace and grows day by day.

Peter visits the city of Lydda, where two men come to find him.

Come quickly to our home in Joppa!

Our sister Tabitha is dead!

She who was so good . . .

And did such good works!

What a traged

Leave me alone with her . . .

Tabitha, get up!

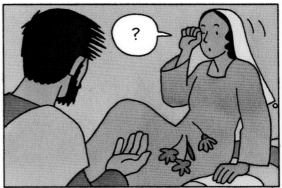

?

The Lord has restored our sister to life!

Glory to God!

After this miracle, many people of Joppa come to believe in the Lord Jesus.

THE BIRTH OF THE CHURCH OF ANTIOCH

Acts 11:19–26

After Stephen's death, many disciples flee, some as far as the city of Antioch, where they continue proclaiming the Gospel.

Jesus is Lord!

Many people are converted. The apostles in Jerusalem hear about it.

Let's send them Barnabas.

On his arrival in Antioch, Barnabas is filled with joy.

It is truly the grace of God at work here!

...d so he encourages ...e new Church:

Brothers, remain faithful to the Lord Jesus with all your heart!

Then he goes to seek Paul in the city of Tarsus.

You'll see, the Lord is working wonders in Antioch!

...or a whole year, Paul and Barnabas help ...build up the Church of Antioch.

Jesus said, "Love your enemies, too . . ."

It is in Antioch that Jesus' disciples are first given the name of "Christians".

GOSPEL VOYAGERS

Acts 13 and 14

The Holy Spirit inspires the Christians of Antioch to send Paul and Barnabas on a mission.

Lord, give them the strength to spread your Gospel wherever they go . . .

Farewell, brothers!

They set off on a ship for the island of Cyprus.

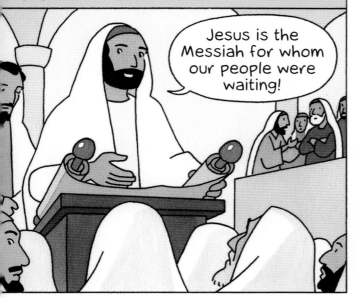

here they proclaim the Word of God in the nagogues.

Jesus is the Messiah for whom our people were waiting!

Then they return to sea, traveling ever farther.

ne day, in the ty of Lystra, Paul eals a man.

I can walk!

It's a miracle!

These men are gods!

Let's offer them a sacrifice!

…the towns they visit, Paul and Barnabas …courage the disciples.

Many hardships await you . . . Stand firm!

They appoint elders* for each of the Churches.

May the Lord help you to care for your brothers . . .

…ter several years …travels:

Antioch, at last!

Paul and Barnabas gather the Christians of Antioch and tell them everything God has done with them.

The door of the faith has been opened to Gentiles!**

Glory to you, Lord!

…ders
…ose who believe in many gods, also called pagans

THE COUNCIL OF JERUSALEM

Acts 15:1–31

In Antioch, more and more Gentiles are converted.

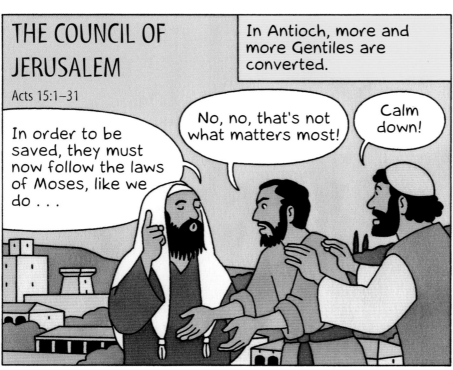

In order to be saved, they must now follow the laws of Moses, like we do . . .

No, no, that's not what matters most!

Calm down!

We must go ask the opinion of Peter and the apostles in Jerusalem . . .

Paul, Barnabas, and a few brothers set off.

In Jerusalem, the Church meets to welcome and consu with them. Peter stands up:

I bear witness that God has grant the Gentiles his Spirit, just as he did He purified them by faith. We used think it was enough to obser the Law to be purified, but it the grace of Jesus that saves Just as it does them .

en Paul and Barnabas tell of the onders of God among the Gentiles.

How extraordinary!

What do you think, James?

I think that if the Gentiles convert, we shouldn't trouble them with laws that aren't theirs. Let's just ask them, out of respect for those who follow the law of Moses, to avoid impure foods and forbidden unions.

You're right.

Judas and Silas will accompany you with this letter.

Back in Antioch, the messengers gather the assembly of the faithful . . .

"Brothers, here is what the Holy Spirit and we have decided . . ."

And all are reassured by their brothers' words of encouragement.

THE PRISONERS FREED

Acts 16:23–34

Paul and Silas travel throughout Macedonia. In Philippi, they are arrested, beaten, and thrown into prison.

Guard them closely!

Near midnight

May my soul live to praise you ♪ ♫

Suddenly:

BA-BOOM!

What's happening?

It's an earthquake!

Waking with a start, the guard panics.

The doors are open! The prisoners must have escaped . . .

So, in the middle of the night, the guard and his whole family are baptized. And they prepare a feast with great rejoicing!

PAUL IN ATHENS

Acts 17:16–34

In the city of Athens, Paul proclaims the Gospel to passers-by.

Before the Areopagus . . .

THE FOUNDING OF THE CHURCH OF CORINTH

Acts 18:1–11 and 1 Corinthians 1:10

Paul arrives in Corinth and meets a couple of Jewish tentmakers.

I'm Aquila, and this is my wife, Priscilla . . .

Did you know this i the trade I learned

Come stay with us, then! There's plenty of work . . .

Paul works with them during the week, and each Sabbath* he speaks in the synagogue.

The Lord is my light ♪ ♩

Jesus is truly the Messiah!

But the Jewish community rises against him.

Liar!

We don't want to hear you anymore!

*The Jewish day of rest and prayer

From now on, I'll go to the Gentiles!

And Paul proclaims the Word in a house next door to the synagogue.

Hearing him speak, many Corinthians, Gentiles and Jews, come to believe and ask to be baptized.

ne night, Paul as a vision:

My Lord!

Do not be afraid, go on speaking! I am with you. Many will come to me in this city . . .

Paul stays a year and a half in Corinth. Later on, he will continue to encourage the Corinthians through his letters.

"Brothers, I ask in the name of Jesus that there be no divisions among you . . ."

PAUL'S FAREWELL TO THE ELDERS

Acts 20:17–38

You know how I wished to serve the Lord humbly among you, despite tears and obstacles. I did everything to teach you, in public and in your homes, inviting Jews and Gentiles alike to be converted and believe in Jesus . . .

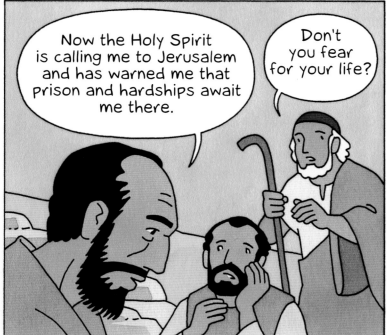

Now the Holy Spirit is calling me to Jerusalem and has warned me that prison and hardships await me there.

Don't you fear for your life?

My life matters little to me! I want only to finish the task I received from the Lord Jesus: to witness to the Gospel . . .

Watch over yourselves and the flock of which the Holy Spirit has made you shepherds.

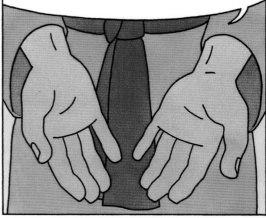

Use your own two hands, as I did, to come to the aid of the weakest! Remember the words of Jesus: "It is more blessed to give than to receive."

Let us pray together, one last time . . .

Then, weeping, they embrace him.

Farewell, dear brother!

And Paul sets sails back to Jerusalem.

FROM JERUSALEM TO ROME

Acts 21:26—28:30

In Jerusalem, Paul goes to the Temple to pray. Suddenly . . .

This man is a traitor!

He goes about speaking ill of our people, the law, and the Temple!

Get out!

Kill him!

Roman soldiers arrive . . .

Go on, move along!

This way, you!

Please let me speak to them . . .

I'm a Jew like you! I know and respect our laws. I hunted down the disciples of Jesus! But one day, on the road to Damascus . . .

And Paul tells about his conversion and how the Lord sent him to the Gentiles. But the crowd goes wild, and the Romans lock Paul up.

That night, the Lord appears to him:

Take courage! You witnessed to me in Jerusalem; you will do the same in Rome . . .

Paul is held prisoner in the city of Caesarea for two years.

The high priests of your people insist that they judge you . . .

I ask to be judged by Caesar.

In Rome? That is your right . . .

A few days later, Paul leaves with other prisoners for Italy.

During the crossing, the ship is caught in a terrible storm.

We're going to die!

Courage, God is watching over us!

Land!

Look out for the rocks!

Jump! We're close to the shore!

CRACK!

We're all alive . . .

Thank the Lord

They remain three months on the island of Ma where Paul heals many sick people.

Then the prisoners arrive in Rome . . .

Are you Paul?

We're Christians!

We heard you had come . . .

Brothers! What joy, Lord!

Until your trial, I allow you to live in the city. A soldier will guard you . . .

For two years, Paul receives all those who come to him, proclaiming to them the kingdom of God and speaking with assurance about Jesus Christ.

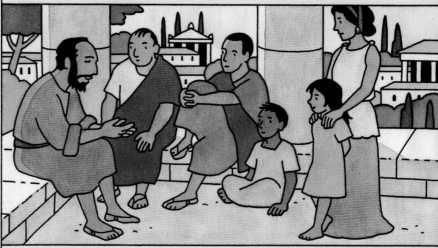

And so, in Rome, the Church grows and becomes strong. It is in this city that Peter, Paul, and many Christians will give their lives for the Gospel.

Original French edition:
Les Actes des Apôtres en bandes dessinées

© 2004 by Fleurus-Edifa, Paris
© 2011 by Ignatius Press, San Francisco • Magnificat USA LLC, New York
All rights reserved
ISBN Ignatius Press 978-1-58617-621-1 • ISBN Magnificat 978-1-936260-14-0

The trademark MAGNIFICAT depicted in this publication is used under license
from and is the exclusive property of Magnificat Central Service Team, Inc.,
A Ministry to Catholic Women, and may not be used without its written consent.

Printed by Tien Wah Press, Malaysia
Printed on February 8, 2011
Job Number MGN 11001